creative Brick

&Stonework

for the Garden

by

Dene Clatworthy

A Devon Craftsman

ISBN 0-9544472-4-7

Unless otherwise stated, all photographs are the copyright of the author

Little Silver Publications
Little Silver Cottage, Matford, Exeter EX2 8XZ

Printed & designed by Sprint Print Co Ltd. Exeter

Contents

**A range of ideas for the garden, using brick and stone.
All the features shown and described in this book were
constructed by the author.**

An oval shaped stone planter in a lovely garden setting *(above)*

A planted wishing well built with natural stone. *(right)*

The Woodcutter's seat *(opposite page)*

This planter has been built with old, reclaimed stock bricks from the east end of London. *(above)*

The lovely deep yellow colour, uneven edges and creased surface give these bricks great character. *(right)*

A circular brick planter within a courtyard setting. *(above)*

A small box-shaped brick planter, with a coping stone finish and a rectangular brick planter with a coping stone finish *(above).*

Wide stone and slab steps, between low level dry stone walls.

Weathered, slightly curved steps built with stone-effect bricks, leading to a raised patio area *(above)*.

Brick and slab steps, built into a steep bank *(above)*.

Steps

Curved stone steps, with built-in planters either side *(above)*.
These steps are built with stone risers and slab treads, and are set between
curved sloping mortared stone walls *(below)*.

This wishing well, with its circular brick bed has been lovingly planted, making it a colourful and attractive feature.

In this courtyard, random size slabs have been laid to form a large patio. The various sizes and weather-worn appearance of the slabs make the area look less uniform, and more in character with the surroundings *(above).*

A face-brick edging *(see next page)* provides a wide solid finish, also matching the brick arches on the house. Rural items and colourful pots make this an attractive feature.

Close up view of the brick edgings shown on the previous page.

In the same garden is a quiet sitting area *(above).*

Patios

A circular, natural stone patio with granite setts forming the outer edge. Being neat and compact, this dainty looking patio can be incorporated into a relatively small area *(above).*

Slab patio with a timber pergola, to encourage climbing plants *(left).*

Low maintenance and practical, slab terraces *(above and below).*

Patios

Random size slab patio *(above)*.

Stone cobbles bedded in mortar provide an in-fill to the out edge of these slabs *(above)*.

Slab patio beside pond and water feature *(above)*.

Slab patio with water feature and arbour seat *(above)*.

Water Features

An attractive, natural stone water feature with a tumbling waterfall effect. The large top cover stone gives the appearance of water flowing from a small cave.

The surrounding area has been set with rockery stones and planted with small shrubs to provide greenery and colour, creating a natural look.

At night, the feature is lit up, giving the whole scene a magical appearance.

Natural stone water feature falling into a pond *(above).*

Small stone water feature *(left).*

A solid, robust table, using hard-wearing weathered York stone for the top and base. The supporting column consists of reclaimed London stock bricks *(above).*

A neat little table, built in face bricks and shaped slabs *(left).*

This *Gold Medal* winning Show Garden was designed and built by the author.

"Moor Besides" is a garden with a West Country theme, inspired by the Dartmoor National Park in Devon. Shapes and curves reflect the contours and undulations of the moor. The garden's design incorporates the various types of local, natural stone to form the traditional dry-stone walls, raised beds and winding path.

The planting evokes a "sense of place". Plants have been chosen for their ability to succeed here, so that the colours, forms and textures of the flowers and foliage pick up and enhance the tones and hues of the stonework. Authentic granite-ware blends naturally to create the true atmosphere of Dartmoor's unique tapestry.

The Winding Path

A different type of Dartmoor stone has been used for each of the stepping stones in the path, which has been designed to wind around towards the seating area, thus adding interest.

Chippings fill the areas around the stones, with granite setts forming the borders.

Surrounding foliage and grass softens the finished effect.

Granite Standing Stone

This granite standing stone, of which there are many on Dartmoor, occupies a corner position in the garden.

The frontal curved tiers of rust-coloured Dartmoor stone have been planted with ferns and rockery plants that soften the feature against the dry stone walling backdrop.

Seating Area

The rustic garden seat, and neutral coloured slabs on a slightly raised seating area, blend in with the surrounding dry stone walls.

The stone shelf built into the dry stone wall makes a delightful and practical feature *(opposite)*.

Ornamental pots and containers can be placed around, some perhaps with suitably aromatic plants.

Granite Water Feature

Water flowing over a piece of Dartmoor granite on a grass mound. The granite has been drilled centrally, with a pump hidden in a reservoir under the stone.

The water flows down the stone, giving a visually pleasing effect.

Old Granite Trough, Planted

An old granite trough can be made an attractive feature when planted up with suitable small alpines and flowers *(below)*.

Granite Staddle Stone

Staddle stones were originally used to support hayricks, allowing ventilation underneath, and preventing rats and other vermin from creating nests in the rick.

Later used to support small barns and outbuildings, staddle stones are now very popular in gardens as ornamental features.

Handsome blue stone pillars, supporting heavy wrought iron gates.

Gate Pillars

These impressive pillars have been built in carefully selected limestone and sand, and completed with pier caps *(above)*.

Simple, but nevertheless attractive face-brick pillars alongside an adjoining wall in the same brick *(above)*.

The Woodcutter's Seat

A large triangular shaped stone provides the back rest for this country-style seat. Reclaimed yellow stock bricks from London form the base, which can also be used as a handy storage area if the seating stone is left unbedded.

The gorgeous colours of the rustic and blue stone stand out on this curved, retaining dry stone wall.

The bank above contains flowers and plants that overhang the top coping stone.

A similar wall *(opposite)* makes this beautiful entrance to the driveway.

Low level retaining dry stone wall with attractive fence above, giving privacy to the garden. *(below).*

Brick and Stone Walling

Various shades of colour in this wall, built with reclaimed bricks.

A very steep grass slope in this garden, proving difficult to maintain, has been overcome by creating tiers with low level, slightly curved dry stone walls.

The little terraces have been laid with chippings, leaving them maintenance-free, or as a flat surface for, perhaps, pots.

Brick and Stone Walling

This charming garden has been created by transforming a grass slope into tiers, using retaining dry stone walls. Steps provide access to a grass path on the middle level, with beautifully planted surrounding beds. At either end, the walling has been curved, softening the overall appearance *(this page and opposite)*.

Brick and Stone Walling

A planting area has been built into the top of this granite wall *(above)*.

A mortared stone wall, forming a raised bed *(above)*.

Face-brick garden walls, with a coping stone finish.

Low level retaining dry stone walls.

Face-brick walling beneath a beautiful Victorian style verandah.

A mortared stone wall, built from locally obtained limestone. The stone has been randomly laid, and the wall forms the boundary on this particular side of the garden.

A mortared stone wall with flower bed *(above)*, alongside a granite chipping driveway.

Foliage growing around trellis fixed to the top of this face-brick wall.

Face-brick garden wall with built-in planters.

Warm, coloured, stone walling *(above)*.

A mortared flint wall *(left)* and retaining a bank using limestone *(below)*.

Sundials have always been a popular garden feature.

Here, one has been constructed using York stone and reclaimed bricks, making a pleasant addition to any garden.

This decorative "figure of eight" shaped path has been laid with a brick edge that defines the curves and boundary between the surrounding shrubs and the path.

It encircles two small trees within flower beds and the walking surface has been laid with slate chippings.

A garden seat occupies a restful position at the end of the path.

Multi-coloured shades of rustic and blue stone make this a colourful path *(left)*.

A practical brick pavoir path allowing easy access from pavement to door *(right)*.

Arbour seat with slab base.

Benches created with Devon stone.

Dry Stone Sculptures

These features can make pleasant "follies" especially when planted with overgrowing and surrounding foliage.

Nooks and crannies in the stone can provide a small haven for wildlife.

An effective focal point can be achieved with a statue or figurine set upon this brick and sandstone slab plinth.

Bird Baths

A simple brick column on which rests a ceramic bird bath.

This feature looks attractive in any garden and will of course, attract many species of wild birds.